A

Compendium

of

Articles

on

Indian Wildlife

by

AQEEL FAROOQI

Contents

TIGER ON THE ROAD ...... *TO EXTINCTION*

(Dec 1998)

The death knell has been sounded, and there remains no doubt that the Indian tiger - that awesome and most beautiful of all cats - is now leaving its last few pugmarks on the short road to extinction. There is a sense of helplessness and desperation in all wildlife lovers about the inevitability of the tiger's extinction, fuelled not by the ever-decreasing number of tigers, but by the seeming lack of concern in this area.

Year after year, optimistic tiger census figures, generated by dubious means, are flaunted at us. If these are to be believed, we have a steady tiger population in the country, one that is not showing a downtrend but actually increasing. On the other hand, the various national and international NGOs, vociferously engaged in a last-ditch battle to save the tiger, are giving it no more than ten years of life in the wilds of India. Their contention is based on the rapidly growing incidence of tiger poaching in and around the various national parks in the country, which is also indicated by seizures of tiger skins and parts all over the country.

The recent spurt in tiger deaths near Corbett & Dudhwa Tiger Reserves have all been attributed to poisoning by villagers who, angry at losing livestock to the great predator, resort to lacing the carcass of the cow or buffalo killed by the tiger with massive doses of pesticide. But does this vile, and purely human instinct for revenge, in any way dilute the ghastly fact that the tigers have been poached? The loss that the entire nation suffers when a tiger is killed is surely far greater than the loss of a cow or buffalo of a poor villager. Whereas giving money to the villager can compensate for cattle killed by the feline, can even one dead tiger be replaced? This 'angry villager' syndrome that we seem to be getting trapped in, will be a welcome smoke-screen for the poacher-trader nexus which is thriving brazenly on tiger bones and parts.

It is quite understandable that a free-ranging cat like the tiger is bound to come in conflict with humans living in the vicinity of its shrinking habitat, and constantly making inroads or trespassing in core areas. It is also reasonable to give concessions to the people for whom saving the tiger and its habitat is just a government job, and a tough one too. But it is not logical for people who commit lapses in their job, to evade responsibility by hiding behind thin veils.

There was one incident in Dudhwa last year, where the killing of a sub-adult tiger, whose body was found in the early stages of decomposition, was explained away by the authorities as death due to an intra-specific fight. Billy Arjan Singh cried himself hoarse in meetings and the newspapers, that it is the rarest of incidents when a tiger will kill another of its own kind, but to no avail. To prove his contention that this tiger had been poached by humans, one activist of the Tiger Haven Wildlife Trust came up with a photograph that showed a homespun rope made out of moonjh grass, knotted around the foreleg of that tiger carcass. **"The big tiger killed this small one, then tied the rope and wanted to drag him away"**, was the wry comment of this activist, who absolutely discarded the 'intra-specific fight' theory.

Earlier, there had been more bizzare explanations, when a spurt of killings saw four tiger carcasses floating in the waterbodies in and around Dudhwa. These were attributed to drowning death by suicide, committed by the tigers following rapid increase in their population. It was hard to visualize Indian tigers behaving like lemmings and jumping into the water to commit suicide, when even a layman could understand that a poisoned tiger, whose trachea is choking in spasms, will rush madly towards water in its death throes, as those poor tigers did.

The need of the hour is honesty. On all sides. This virtue, which most of us today don't consider worth passing on to our children, is what the tiger desperately needs, if at all it is to be saved. The forest officials, on their part, must come forward and admit tiger deaths that are caused due to poaching, rather than trying to evade responsibility by evolving ridiculous explanations for them.

Once a tiger death due to poaching is accepted, and the acceptance is backed up by the firm commitment to overcome the lapse, it would become that much easier to go all out in evolving and implementing effective damage-control measures. Otherwise, the forest department's folly will always be evident to others, even though ostrich-like, it may have hidden its head under some convenient, but unlikely, explanation.

On the other hand, there is the growing tendency of non-official conservationists to lay the entire blame on the forest department officials without taking cognizance of their limitations in terms of staff, equipment and commitment.

That is the basic reason why these two protagonists, playing out the drama of the tiger's extinction, are constantly at loggerheads. And so, while they keep their horns locked in adversarial contest, vital time is going waste, and nothing concrete is being done. Forest criminals and tiger poachers are having a field day. Trees are being felled to fuel illegal activities of the timber mafia, while tigers are being regularly killed for their skins and bones, which pass through greased palms, and find their way into countries like China, to be sold for astonishing sums in the black market.

The saddest part of this tragic drama is that the focus of the tiger killers has now shifted to Corbett National Park, which was till now considered the best managed tiger reserve, and enjoyed a certain level of immunity from the poacher -- more because of its geographic layout than any human efficiency. But having drastically depleted the tiger population of Dudhwa & Ranthambore, the poachers have now turned towards the relatively healthier tiger population of Corbett Park.

Recent reports in the media have placed the tiger deaths in Corbett at around five in less than a month, even as meetings were being held at the highest levels to mark the Year of the Tiger, and the **'experts'** were congratulating themselves on the formation of some committee or the other to save the tiger. In one fell stroke, the tiger killers had brought to naught all that these committees stand for, and shattered the mythical impregnability of Corbett Tiger Reserve. This, more than anything else, sounds like the death knell.

Much has already been written and said about the inevitability of the tiger's extinction from India, but it still doesn't seem enough to jerk us out of apathy. The recent tiger killings in Corbett, and a glance at hard statistics given in the table*, indicating both optimistic and pessimistic world population estimates, will surely make the reader understand that ten, or even a lesser number of years, are all that remain for the Indian tiger in the wild. The experts don't deny that most tiger census figures are educated guesses, and so it is for the reader to strike that delicate balance between the optimistic and pessimistic estimates of the tiger population.

But whichever way we look at it, if the present downtrend is not arrested, the tiger will fade away into oblivion, and we would be left handling nothing but statistics of what is probably the greatest Indian heritage.

WORLD TIGER POPULATION AT A GLANCE			
Tiger	**Subspecies**	**Min**	**Max**
1.Bengal tiger P.t. tigris		3,030	4,735
	Bangladesh	300	460
	Bhutan	50	240
	China	30	35
	India	2,500	3,750
	Nepal	150	250
2.Caspian tiger **Extinct in 1970s** P.t.virgata	Formerly in Afghanistan, Iran, Turkestan, Turkey		
3.Siberian tiger P.t.altaica (Amur/Ussuri/North-East China/Manchurian)		447	505
	China	20	12
	Korea (North)	< 10	< 10
	Russia	425	475
4. Javan tiger P.t. sondaica **Extinct in 1980s**			
5. South China (Amoy) tiger P.t. amoyensis		20	30
6. Bali tiger **Extinct in 1940s** P.t.balica			
7.Sumatran tiger P.t.sumatrae		400	500
8. Indo-Chinese tiger P. t. corbetti		1180	1790
	Cambodia	100	200
	China	30	40
	Malaysia	600	650
	Thailand	250	600
	Vietnam	200	300
World Totals		**5,077**	**7,560**

STATE DEVELOPMENT PROJECT
THREATENS STATE BIRD – SARUS
June 26, 2001

More than once, avid tiger-lovers from foreign countries have accosted me with the rueful complaint that although we Indians have declared the tiger as our national animal, we are doing precious little to save it from being decimated by poachers. The ever-increasing frequency of seizures of tiger bones and skins in recent times is such overwhelming evidence that it precludes any argument to the contrary. And so, while one falters for a convincing answer, the question that really nags is whether we actually seek to destroy what we revere, or is it just inherent callousness that leaves us untouched by our collective depredations against nature and its bounties.

If India as a country stands accused of failure to protect the national animal, the state of Uttar Pradesh is now on the verge of being indicted in the same manner for threatening the very existence of the state bird Sarus, in the districts of Etawah and Mainpuri where it has been apparently flourishing.

Of the three sub-species of this tallest flying bird in the world, the Indian Sarus is the largest and is distributed in Pakistan, Nepal, India and Bangladesh. According to researchers, the global population estimate of the subspecies is between 8,000–1,000, with more than 95% spread across India.

But it is Uttar Pradesh that has the distinction of being home to more than 50% of the total Indian population of Sarus, which probably was reason enough for the thoughtful state government to accord it the honourable status of 'state bird'. The highest number and density of Sarus is found in the districts of Etawah and Mainpuri, which provide an excellent habitat due to the existence of a number of marshlands, most suited to the nesting and breeding of this bird. The border areas of these two districts encompassing the towns of Etawah, Saiphai, Karhal, Saman, Sarsai Nawar, and Baralokpur contain a substantial population, with the highest numbers being concentrated in four wetlands - Kudaiyya & Ambarpur in Mainpuri, Saman Katra lying in Mainpuri / Etawah, and Sarsai Nawar in Etawah.

Ironically however, it is a development project of the Ministry of Agriculture, aimed at enhancing the agricultural area of Etawah & Mainpuri, envisages the draining out of a number of these wetlands, thereby threatening to destroy crucial habitat for Sarus as well as other birds, plants and animals. It is rather unfortunate that the Ministry for Rural Development has categorized wetlands and marshlands as **'wastelands'** even though these are globally regarded as endangered habitats having tremendous biodiversity, as well as being of crucial importance in hydrological cycles. It is understood that the Ministry of Agriculture project plans to reclaim these wetlands under 'wasteland development'. It goes without saying that if the implementation of this plan goes on, it may cause irreparable displacement of a great number of Sarus populations in the area, leading to huge declines in the productivity of breeding pairs.

It is to the credit of the state government that ornithologists and conservationists concede that while wetlands are persecuted without a second thought all over the country, Uttar Pradesh has so far succeeded in preserving most of its wetlands. If this sense of confidence is to be retained, it would be incumbent upon the state government to review the present project in the light of the Environment Impact Analysis which must surely have been prepared before its implementation.

This is not to say that development activity for humans should be side-lined, but only that it must go on without destroying other species. Researchers and conservation NGO's have been working overtime to bring alternative strategies before the government, which can be adopted to save the Sarus without hurdling the developmental project. It is now up to the planners and officials to take bold decisions to help the Sarus survive where it belongs.

Few people in their forties and more, can forget the ubiquitous Sarus during their younger days, when not a single train or road journey could end without the sighting of this magnificent bird in the countryside. They would also remember the many legends told of its undying loyalty to its mate, which seemed to be the key virtue that earned it our respect and awe. For the sake of the Sarus cranes of Etawah and Mainpuri, I can only hope that the planners and officials belong to that age and time.

SHAHTOOSH BAN GAINS MOMENTUM WORLDWIDE

July 4, 2001

If the Tibetan people, as a nation, have to take up cudgels against the occupation of their country by a larger and more powerful neighbour, there also exists a native animal species in the country – the Tibetan antelope - which perforce has to wage a last ditch-battle against its very extermination at the hands of a more formidable foe – the international poacher. And the only reason why this animal is so ruthlessly persecuted is that its fur unfortunately yields the highest quality of wool ever known to man.

The Tibetan antelope, Pantholops hodgsoni, also known as the 'chiru,' is now found only in the remote plateaus of Tibet, and the Xinjiang, and Qinghai provinces of China. It is estimated that the chiru population ran into several million at the turn of the 20th century, during which time they were also known to converge in the valleys of northern Laddak, but their population has now alarmingly dropped to less than 75,000 today. Wildlife biologists and conservationists aver that chiru are currently being illegally hunted at the rate of 20,000 per year for their wool, commonly known as 'shahtoosh' (king of wools, in Persian). The slaughtered animals end up supplying a high fashion trade of fine, soft shawls made from their wool. Sold in fashion outlets in New York, Paris, London, and Hong Kong, these shawls generate thousands of dollars each, from buyers who are often unaware that they are obtaining a product which is illegal internationally.

13

Tibetan antelope are protected under Appendix I of the Convention on International Trade in Endangered Species (CITES), which prohibits any trade in their products, worldwide. They have also been given Class I protection status under China's Wildlife Laws, while in India they are listed in Schedule 1 of The Wildlife (Protection) Act, 1972, at par with the tiger, elephant and other highly endangered species.

The high rate of decimation of chirus at the hands of poachers and traders has now galvanized the international conservation community to plunge headlong into the battle to save the species. In India, the Wildlife Protection Society of India (WPSI), the WWF-India and the Wildlife Trust of India (WTI) have all made significant contributions to its conservation. Whereas WPSI took the issue of shahtoosh to court and was instrumental in obtaining a restraint order from the Jammu High Court against the use of shahtoosh as material for the making of shawls by Kashmiri weavers, the WTI collaborated with the International Fund for Animal Welfare (IFAW) to conduct an in-depth investigation of the illegal trade in Tibetan antelope wool.

On June 27th, 2001 IFAW and the WTI held simultaneous press conferences in London, Beijing, and New Delhi, and announced the results of the joint investigation that revealed the international scope of the highly illegal trade in Tibetan antelope wool from China and shawls from India – a trade, which the report says, may cause the extinction of this unique species within the next five years.

According to the report entitled, "Wrap Up the Trade - An International Campaign to Save the Endangered Tibetan Antelope", the raw shahtoosh wool is smuggled into India, ending up in the state of Jammu and Kashmir where it is woven into high quality shawls, which continue to be sold illegally to the wealthy elite in countries such as the UK, USA, Italy and France. The investigation lasted for over eight months, and was carried out by five teams in three countries. The teams collected first-hand information and video footage of the illegal trade of chiru pelts being carried on in the border areas between China, Nepal and India. For added measure, they also conducted a socio-economic survey of an estimated 30,000 shahtoosh workers to determine possible impacts of a ban on shahtoosh weaving in the state of Jammu and Kashmir.

Fortunately, in India, it seems that the awareness of the illegality of shahtoosh shawls has been hammered home, and hopefully the elite class that can afford to buy one, will now have nothing to do with such a shawl. Moreover, with Mrs Maneka Gandhi recently prevailing upon the outgoing US ambassador's wife to disown the shahtoosh shawl in her possession, the media attention and the subsequent discussions about the event in high-fashion circles must surely have helped to cement the point.

But the all-important question which remains to be answered is whether the illegal wildlife trade in India will cease to deal in shahtoosh, since it is inextricably linked to the trade in tiger parts, whereby traffickers supplying illegal tiger parts from India to China, trade them for Tibetan antelope pelts or wool, which are so highly sought this side of the border. And going by the massive seizures of tiger skins and bones made by the STF in Uttar Pradesh recently, it is evident that the wildlife traffickers in the state have been actively carrying on their sinister enterprise. In most of these seizures, it was determined by the STF sleuths that the tiger skins and bones were destined for Nepal, and possibly onward to China for use in the traditional medicines which that country is so infamous for.

There is no doubt that shahtoosh would have been one of the prizes gleefully bartered by the traders in exchange of the tiger derivatives. A fair exchange, one would wryly admit. Hardly ironical then, that the Indian tiger and Tibetan antelope are both listed in the same Schedule 1 of the Wildlife (Protection) Act.

THE ROAD TO DISASTER

July 11, 2001

With the cleaving out of Uttaranchal from the state of Uttar Pradesh, the long-standing aspirations of its people to acquire statehood for their region, may have been fulfilled. But in doing so, the political scythe unwittingly inflicted the unkindest cut on countless people like me, who prided themselves on being denizens of a state which boasted of such wild havens as Dudhwa, Corbett and Rajaji national parks, not to speak of a lofty mountain range within which nestled many other places of greater pristine grandeur.

If forfeiting its green crown was a great loss to Uttar Pradesh, the fledgling state found itself flush with a relatively high percentage of forest cover, and a rich biodiversity that came along with it. From the wildlife conservationists' viewpoint, the new state has inherited this immense forest wealth not for exploitation or financial gain, but as a natural heritage that is sacrosanct, and to be honestly preserved. No doubt there exists the need for the new state to enhance basic infrastructure like roads, to set the pace for economic development and self-sustenance in vital sectors like transport and tourism, on which it is heavily dependent. But this development has to be carried out carefully, without inviting opposition from environmental groups and activists who are of the focused view that they would blow the whistle on any large-scale developmental activity in Uttaranchal, if it is carried out without taking environmental concerns into account

17

As it happened, one of the first few developmental projects of the government turned out to be a highly contentious issue. This project involved the construction of a proposed highway from Kotdwar to Kalagarh and on to Ramnagar, on an existing route alignment that passed through the Corbett Tiger Reserve along its southern boundary, with several stretches of the planned road traversing the core areas of the tiger reserve between Khara Gate and Kalagarh town, while the remainder largely running through the buffer zone.

As expected, the conservationists were up in arms and managed to get a stay order from the Supreme Court in April last. The order was passed during proceedings in an ongoing PIL on tiger conservation, when Solicitor General Harish Salve mentioned an interim application submitted by the Wildlife Protection Society of India (WPSI), which clearly outlined the apprehension that such a high way through the Corbett Tiger Reserve would be disastrous for wildlife, bringing in its wake a high frequency of heavy vehicular movement, proliferation of road-side establishments for food and vehicular maintenance, thereby causing noise and disturbance levels to reach mind-boggling levels in this hitherto prime wildlife habitat.

Thanks to the Supreme Court directives, the highway construction has been stayed for the moment, but it is far from being a permanent solution to the problem. Considering that road transport is the key to development, it is understandable that the compulsive road building activity of the Uttaranchal government is ostensibly guided by the objective that movement of commercial vehicles within the state should be made possible without them having to criss-cross through Uttar Pradesh roads. To create such a road network would necessitate new route alignments. At present however, the existing road network makes it incumbent upon vehicles plying between far-flung origins and destinations within Uttaranchal, to make use of roads lying in UP jurisdiction - and thereby becoming liable for payment of various taxes that accrue to the UP Transport department.

This dual taxation, as well as the compulsion to traverse longer distances on circuitous routes through UP, had become a point of contention for Uttaranchal transporters, and the need to provide them solace in this regard must have been the priority which determined the state government's decision to go ahead with the highway construction. It is another matter however, that the glee with which this remedy was sought to be applied, points to the tremendous benefits that lie in store for contractors and the timber industry through the execution of such projects. This can be gauged by the fact that by the time the stay was ordered, around 7000 trees had already been felled in the process. It is this unholy speed which is blatantly exhibited in implementation of destructive projects which raises doubts and questions. It also reinforces the fear that if this project had been allowed to go on without taking environmental concerns into account, the process of planning and executing more road projects in the future, would leave more and more Uttaranchal Forest areas susceptible to felling and encroachments.

If the solution to this problem had been sought with environmental concerns – and not "developmental" ones -

being paramount, it might have been a good idea for the Central government to arbitrate between the UP & Uttaranchal governments, and enforce either some kind of a moratorium or waiver of this dual taxation, or maybe effect an increase in the number of kms which a vehicle is allowed to traverse in another state without inviting taxation – if its origin and destination is within its state. Calculated based on state's annual revenue, this financial setback may undeniably amount to a sizeable sum, but in the long run it would still be too little as compared to the massive environmental degradation we may suffer at the hands of faulty planning at this stage.

Although the highway construction has been stayed for the moment, it should not be forgotten that that its planning and execution was bad in law, otherwise it would never have invited the attention of the Supreme Court. The significance of the Supreme Court stay order lies in the fact that for the time being the road cannot be constructed even in the reserve forest land, as has been proposed by the state government. Initially, the Centre had approved the proposed highway under the Forest Conservation Act 1980, provided no part of the road went through the national park area.

However, the three-judge bench comprising Justice A.S. Anand, Justice R.C Lahoti and Justice Brijesh Kumar clarified in their order that the stay would not hinder the Uttaranchal government as long as the road did not pass through the tiger reserve.

It is now up to the development agencies in the state to take advantage of the considered view of the Supreme

Court ruling and reconsider this problem with a holistic approach to seek a solution that does not disregard environmental and wildlife conservation issues.

WARRING NGO'S MAY SPELL DOOM FOR THE TIGER

July 18, 2001

If a disagreement on a mere choice of words can bring a summit of nations to naught, it would hardly come as a surprise that a difference of opinion, an altercation, or maybe plain mutual dislike between the heads of two leading Indian conservation NGO's should be enough to jeopardize the very future of the Indian tiger, which ostensibly is so pivotal to the fulfilment of the avowed objectives that these NGO's stand for. According to a recent media report, an "ugly spat" between the CEO of WWF-India and the Director of Traffic-India has prompted the parent body WWF-International, to put its Tiger Conservation Programme (TCP) on hold for the moment, and freeze all its conservation related funds to WWF-India. This, if effected for any measure of time, would mean that all conservation activities in India which are presently being funded by the WWF would come to an abrupt standstill, thereby causing the tiger to become the direct casualty.

The need for delving into the reasons and intricacies that may have been responsible for bringing the concerned NGO's to such a head, hardly seems to be of any importance since it is not likely that they would go much beyond an ego or personality clash. However, the ramifications and the cascading effect this would have on the plight of the Indian tiger are more critical, and it would be more worthwhile to look at conservation areas that are likely to suffer a negative impact due to this stringent action by WWF.

The extent of the reach and benefits of the Tiger Conservation Programme to the Indian conservation effort can be gauged by the fact that it is possibly the largest funded campaign by an NGO in India which is aimed at conserving an endangered species. It does this by contributing substantially towards augmenting and strengthening the management of tiger reserves in cooperation with the central government and the state governments in which these reserves are located. The material help is provided in the form of much-needed equipment like communication sets, vehicles, boats etc, while direct financial support is also extended to park managements in cases where expedient funds are required.

It also contributes, directly or indirectly, to counter illegal trade in tiger parts through the creation of a network of informers in sensitive areas and passing on this information to enforcement agencies for them to make seizures. Research projects and studies are funded for assessment and monitoring of tiger habitats, and funding schemes are instituted in tiger reserve areas with the intention of reducing human-tiger conflict through payment of compensation for cattle-killing by tigers. TCP also funds and arranges legal support to defend field personnel who are taken to court for their tiger conservation work, and further catalyses the motivation of committed field personnel by instituting and distributing awards for special contributions made by them in the field of tiger conservation. It goes without saying that these activities, funded out of the TCP, go a long way in indirectly fulfilling the budgetary shortfalls which park managements are constantly faced with due to the paucity of finances at the disposal of state governments.

On the other hand, Traffic (Trade Records Analysis of Flora and Fauna in Commerce) is a joint programme of Worldwide Fund for Nature (WWF) and International Union for the Conservation of Nature (IUCN), operating through its various country offices throughout the world. In our country, Traffic-India has been acting as the wildlife trade monitoring arm of WWF-India, with the broad goal of curbing illegal wildlife trade dealing in animal and plant derivatives. It does this through wildlife trade studies, field investigations in support of enforcement agencies, creation of a database relevant to wildlife trade in India, and arranging of training for the country's enforcement agencies for combating wildlife crimes.

Therefore, a properly dove-tailed execution of their programmes and schemes makes both WWF-India and Traffic-India essential to the long-term survival of the Indian tiger. But in this worst-case scenario, if the are to come to loggerheads and become locked in adversarial combat due to the falling out of individuals who have been placed at the helm to provide direction and leadership to these organizations, it would be the worst comment on their commitment and resolve to save the tiger.

It can surely be conceded that with the huge amount of funds being brought into the country from international donors, tiger conservation in India has become big business. It is not surprising then, that these donor agencies sometimes have to organize their activities on corporate principles, including the not so healthy ones like competition and survival. But if they pause to consider the adverse impact this tends to have on the tiger in the field, they should be prepared to take some of the blame for the steady loss of tiger numbers in India, which is painfully highlighted by the increasing frequency of seizures of tiger skins and bones from all across the country. A blame that is today being conveniently passed off entirely on to the hapless state forest departments.

KILLING NILGAIS IN THE NAME OF CROP PROTECTION

Aug 8, 2001

When the Government of Maharashtra recently took the decision of allowing the killing of nilgai (*Boselaphus tragocamelus*) and wild boar (*Sus scrofa*) on the grounds of crop protection, it was merely following what Uttar Pradesh and Madhya Pradesh had already done earlier. Protests from conservationists who were present during the meeting of the Maharashtra state Wildlife Advisory Board were strong, but in the end the interests of man over animal were considered paramount, and the order was passed.

In Uttar Pradesh, the primary man-animal conflict that is of any noticeable dimension is the damage to agricultural fields by herds of crop-raiding nilgai. This is one wild species that has been sustaining its population all over the state due to its relatively higher fecundity, as well as its propensity to survive in agricultural areas, even though its natural habitat has been consistently whittled down to negligible proportions. One important factor that contributed to the nilgai's wide spread survival in the state was the religious reverence in which it used to be held by a large section of the populace. This was the reason why it enjoyed some sort of immunity from large-scale decimation, even though its consistent depredations against farmers made them look upon it as a pest. It did however, prompt them and their elected representatives to keep up a continuous clamour asking the state government to intervene and provide them saccour. In the absence of any other viable measures of crop protection which could be resorted to by farmers, the government had to give in to the demand to allow these raiding animals to be officially killed by hunters.

But from a purely official standpoint, government may receive a very few applications requesting for permission to eliminate raiding nilgais, hence the total number of such animals killed officially would be quite low. This apparently stems from the long-drawn procedure involved in obtaining a permit for elimination, with its concomitant riders like issue of permit only to a rifle license holder, the specific location where the shot can be taken, and the subsequent handing over of the carcass to the department, since according to Section 11 of the Wildlife (Protection) Act, any animal killed in the name of self-defence or crop protection is government property. Moreover, no hunter worth his salt and spices would like to see his booty burning on a pyre prepared by the Forest department, rather than be cooked on a fire of his own making.

But this is not to say that this lack of official implementation of the government's proposed measures to provide relief to farmers, is going in favour of the nilgai. There are enough renegade farmer-hunters who are tackling this issue of crop-protection on their own terms and agenda. Their .315's and 12 bores have always been lending loud support to this huge public outcry against the depredations of the nilgai. Their tractors and trolleys are used to bring in the crop during the day, while at night they bring home the crop-raiders. The more modest ones are silently pegging away with their wire-snares, sulphas tablets concealed in guavas, and deadly electrocution lines tapped off from high-tension cables. The nilgais they bring down will never be counted in any

official record.

The graphic educational campaign carried out in the state highlighting the reasons why a nilgai was not a 'cow', and officially renaming it as 'vanroz', has the dubious distinction of being a huge success in converting some peoples' reverence into abhorrence, and ultimately adding to the numbers of the bloodthirsty lot. The poor wild boar, another wild species considered as a crop pest, was already on the 'hate list' of some, and being dealt with accordingly.

And so, there is a real fear in the minds of conservationists that it may just be a matter of time when the ill effects of unregulated and unofficial implementation of a studied government policy will take a heavy toll on their populations, making these two species jump back and forth within the limited Schedules of the Wildlife (Protection) Act.

WHERE HAVE ALL THE SPARROWS GONE?

Aug 22, 2002

The threat to species continues. As the inexorable juggernaut of human development rolls on, it leaves little or no elbowroom for other life forms to cling on tenaciously to the thread of survival. Whether it is the forest or urban environs, so many species are being pushed surely and steadily over the brink of extinction that one now tends to lose count. Although the larger and more well recognized endangered species have strong conservation groups supporting their struggle for existence, but for commoner species these threats are so imperceptible that conservationists get the chance of ringing the warning bells only a long after the damage is done.

One victim of these imperceptible threats is *Passer domesticus*, the common house sparrow. As its name suggests, it is one of the bird species that have always been closely associated with us in our urban environment. A bird so ubiquitous, that it had almost become a part of our lives. More often than not, it was the sparrow which was the 'chiya' that parents pointed out to the bubbly infant in their arms - sometimes as the first lesson in making him aware of the wonders of his new world, or as a distraction to stop his streaming tears when he cried inconsolably in anger or in pain. As he grew up, they regaled him with stories of 'chiriya-chidda', in which the central characters were none other than sparrows.

Our homes always had sparrows as co-habitants. Any wooden rafter, crevice in the wall or the cup in the ceiling fan, was confidently staked by the sparrow to build its nest. Its initial forays, when it was searching for a nest-site, were strongly repulsed. But once it succeeded in laying its claim to a nesting site, we tended to let it go on unhindered. Although it turned out to be a nuisance for the house mistress because of the wispy nest material falling all over the place, it was tolerated with good humour since it contained eggs, and to demolish it was anathema to most. Later, as the hatchlings emerged, they often wriggled too vigorously in their quest for food and fell out of the nests, but were promptly replaced by us with tenderness and care. The ones that didn't survive found teary eyes and willing little hands that laid them gently to rest in impromptu graves dug in the backyard.

But all that is now a thing of the past. Our homes are now drearily silent without the twitter and chirrup of the sparrows, which seem to have either gone into oblivion or have forsaken us in our mad race in the material world. With our beautifully constructed houses and rooms of isolation, we effectively banished the sparrow from our environs. The older generation, for whom feeding the birds was akin to puja, has mostly passed away. The younger generation, with its hard-working couples in single unit families, has neither the time nor the inclination to bother about such mundane distractions as putting out food for the birds. Besides, thanks to the fridge and the changed culinary setup, nothing qualifies as leftovers.

And so, with no food and no place to qualify as home, the poor sparrow has all but made a quiet exit from our lives. Only a few die-hard stragglers remain, to make us more acutely aware of their plight. There may not be any research conducted, and no questions may be asked to explain this loss. After all, the sparrow does not have any NGO rooting for its survival as there are for other high-profile species.

But to those of us who grew up chasing sparrows during the hot summer afternoons, after making stealthy escapes from strictly enforced siestas, the cheerful chirrup from even one sparrow today is enough to gladden our hearts.

CUCKOOS THAT FLY OUT OF CROWS' NESTS

Aug 29, 2001

When August comes, it is time for the urban birdwatcher to regale himself with the drama of the crow and the koel, and witness the humbling of the wily crow by a more cunning adversary. In most areas that have tall eucalyptus or gulmohar trees, it is an interesting sight to see a few pairs of common crows (Corvus splendens) busily feeding raucous young ones of the koel (Eudynamys scolopacea).

To the discerning eye, the differences in the parents and the chicks are vividly marked as far as their appearances and the sounds are concerned, but these do not seem to matter at all for the crows. To their parenting instinct, it is enough to know that the squawky little fledglings, consistently clamouring for food, came out from their nests and hence are nothing but their own brood. More often than not, such a brood may not contain even a single crow chick because nature ensures that the larger size and early hatching ability of the parasitic bird results in the host losing its own clutch, and raising only the young of the parasitic bird.

This then, is a classic example of nest and brood parasitism exhibited in some birds. It is a remarkable reproductive strategy in which one species - the brood parasite – does not build its own nest, but chooses to lay its eggs in the nest prepared by another species. It is this host species that hatches the eggs and later raises the brood parasite's young to adulthood.

The hosts of brood parasites do exhibit some initial defence mechanisms against the usurping of their nests. They may resort to either camouflage or concealment of their nests, or else guarding them aggressively by constantly chasing possible intruders from the vicinity of the nest. But ironically, it is this aggressive behaviour of nesting crows that is easily transformed into successful egg-laying by the koel. As the irritated female crow dashes madly after the male koel that has been ceaselessly needling her while she sits in her nest, the female koel quickly slips into the vacated nest and lays her clutch. She may, if she gets the time, push out some of the crow eggs, but her primary concern is to lay her own before the female crow returns. This done, she quietly flits away to leave the nest back in the possession of the rightful owner, returning triumphantly from the chase.

It is obvious that the female crow is not able to distinguish either the koel's eggs from its own, or notice the change in their numbers after the koel has added her clutch to the nest. This shows that although the crow is universally regarded as a cunning bird it certainly is naïve when it comes to counting chicks before they are hatched. Taking all the eggs in the nest as being their own, both parents continue to hatch them. Later, when the chicks emerge, they too are not recognized as imposters but raised by the crows as their own. Being early hatchers, the koel chicks usually emerge before the crow chicks, and in the process negate any chance for the crow eggs in the nest to hatch. Feeding these ravenous chicks is the only duty that the crows can perform for the next few weeks. Even if a crow chick does manage to hatch, it is usually bullied to starvation by its larger foster sibling. That is the reason why one may not come across a crow pair feeding a joint brood containing both crow and koel chicks. It is probably when the young koels are grown and ready to fly away to an absolutely different tune, that the stumped foster parents realize the goof-up.

One may wonder ceaselessly at the sequence of events that go into this unique natural phenomenon but the cycle of life goes on happily for the crow and the koel. Both species are proving to be quite successful breeders, as is evident by their healthy numbers in our midst. Which unfortunately, is not what we can say for too many species anymore.

CORBETT PARK WOES CONTINUE TO MOUNT

September 5, 2001

Last week's deadly attack by suspected poachers, which took the life of a Deputy Range Officer, and left three other forest guards shot and injured, has added a serious dimension to the escalating threat facing both the wildlife and staff of Corbett Tiger Reserve. Before this blatant attack on the staff of the tiger reserve, the poachers' depredations had been targeting the predominant wildlife species, with elephants being in sharp focus during recent times. But the tragic turn of events in this particular incident are stark indicators that poaching gangs and forest mafia in Uttaranchal have now become so confident and cocksure about their immunity that they would not hesitate to carry out even a frontal attack on forest guards who try to counter their nefarious designs.

The genesis for this heightened disregard for the law among these criminals is not far to seek. Recent events of elephant poaching in the park, and the subsequent failure of enforcement agencies to make any worthwhile investigations or arrests, could well be the *raison d'etre* for the present set of poachers to act with such impunity.

Readers may recall that this year started on a dismal note for Corbett, with as many as six tuskers being expertly killed by a poaching gang operating within the core areas of the park. If recent memory serves one right, there had never been such a concerted onslaught of elephant poaching anywhere in India, as was mounted on the hapless wild elephants of Corbett Tiger Reserve during January & February this year. The modus operandi, and the rapidity with which the poachers were able to strike at elephants deep within the reserve, was proof enough that they were quite skilled in their gruesome craft. They undoubtedly had a clear lay of the terrain as well as the requisite firepower, since it took them less than three hours to shoot an elephant, follow its death trail, and then hack away its tusks.

It all started in October 2000 when one elephant was killed near Gairal, in the northern part of the Reserve. No one took that incident as the precursor of the carnage that was to follow. Taking a cue from the lack of any worthwhile enforcement, the poachers struck again in the last week of December 2000, killing two male elephants in quick succession - one in the Jhirna range and the other near Bijrani. They then followed it up by killing three more tuskers within the first ten days of February.

Unfortunately, the poachers were not countered with any successful enforcement measures. Although the park was closed to visitors and a huge combing operation launched, not a single poacher could be nabbed. In the initial confusion, even the method employed in killing the elephants was not properly established. This was obvious in media reports, where the cause of the pachyderms' death was ascribed to ingestion of 'nails & shrapnel' reportedly fed by the poachers to the elephants concealed in balls of wheat flour laced with jaggery. One wondered even at that time how an intelligent and 'masticating' animal like the elephant could be fed with such a 'loaded' meal, however enticingly it may have been camouflaged. But the reports were graphic in their description of shrapnel found in the elephants' dung, and blood trails on the forest paths, caused by rectal bleeding of the unfortunate animals whose intestines were all cut up presumably by the hardware they had eaten. Other possible causes – like poison or gun, were either not looked for, or even considered.

It was only the post-mortem examination of the latter victims which helped in ascertaining that the death blow was delivered by a poisoned steel rod approximately 7 cm long, shaped like a file fixed in a wooden base. Fired from a muzzle-loading gun, the metal rod generated enough velocity to penetrate the muscle tissues. The elephants fled on being hit, but the debilitating effects of the poison ensured that they did not make much ground before dying. The poachers followed and hacked away at the face after cutting away the trunk, to extract every inch of the tusks from their base.

I am sure that the gruesome photograph of a gentle forest giant, killed and maimed by poachers just for a few kilos of ivory, will bring out in stark detail, the horror and vileness which is being perpetrated on our wildlife by poachers all over the country. If it helps to motivate even a single member of the services, the judiciary or the public at large to join the fight to save our last remaining forests and wildlife, this elephant may not have died in vain.

A QUESTION ON POST MORTEMS IN THE WILD

September 12, 2001

In my humble opinion, over-eating is an indulgence that is exclusively practiced by gastronomes belonging to the human race. But when it comes to animals in the wild, nature and instinct ensures that they eat only the amount that is required for survival. So when the cause of death of the wild elephant that was found dead last week in the forests of Bijnor district, was attributed to over-eating, one tended to reach out for the proverbial pinch of salt.

As the veterinary experts who examined the body of the elephant would have us believe, a perfectly healthy 35-year-old wild tusker suddenly decided to go on an eating spree and ended up dead, entangling all his intestines in the process. The presence of tusks in the carcass, and the lack of any external injury on its body, must have acted as the obvious factors that guided the post-mortem report to discard the hand of the poacher in the death of this elephant. But the logical question that follows is whether the post-mortem examination categorically ruled out the not-so-obvious poisoning as one of the other possible causes?

From an official standpoint, it is understandable that conceding another success to poachers at a time when the Corbett authorities are reeling under the impact of negative publicity, is an entirely avoidable issue. But it should not be forgotten that in the light of the state government's drive for transparency, conservation NGO's and interested members of

38

the public would now tend to show increased desire to be informed of details of hitherto unquestioned departmental activities like disposal of carcasses of poached animals, and details of their post-mortem reports. It would therefore be advisable for the wildlife authorities to conduct these activities with a holistic approach so that if logical and pertinent questions are raised, they may be answered with candidness and clarity.

It may be recalled that the death of a tiger in Pilibhit early this year, and its subsequent post mortem report, had kicked up a lot of controversy about the cause of death. Whereas the official version established it as septicaemia, it was hotly argued by others on the grounds that it was actually a bullet that had injured the tiger in the upper neck region. Being unable to lick itself at the point of injury, it was inevitable that the wound turned gangrenous, and the tiger died of septicaemia. However, the official version stood strong since the Indian Veterinary Research Institute (IVRI) veterinarians who conducted the autopsy clearly ruled out a bullet injury.

A similar debate also arose in Bandhavgarh national park last year, where the post mortem report on a tiger found dead, certified that it had died of over-eating. What prompted the debate was the fact that the tiger had vomited soon after taking a second meal from a kill it had made earlier. These circumstances certainly did not rule out the possibility of poachers having laced the kill with poison. But in that case too, the cause of death that prevailed, was over-eating.

There is no denying the fact that the controversies that are raised in such cases are sometimes the handiwork of disgruntled locals who have an axe to grind against the concerned park management. They also manage to garner the support of local media, which lends credence to the doubts they raise. The only way these doubts can be set at rest is for the authorities to bring in transparency in the conduct of post mortems, especially in cases where the hand of the poacher can even remotely be suspected. Such cases should be examined in the presence of a few knowledgeable members of the public and the media. Once this practice is established, it would greatly help to stop the canards from flying – hopefully from both sides.

But the question that nags, and still remains unanswered, is whether wild animals die of over-eating. And if they do, what sudden physiological impulse overrides their strong natural instinct of equilibrium?

IS IT TIME TO 'CRY WOLF' AGAIN?

September 19, 2001

When the cherubic Little Red Riding Hood made her escape from the snapping jaws of the big bad wolf masquerading as her grandmother, it was inevitable that the dread value of the wolf generated by the fable, would continue to haunt the minds of little children even after they had grown up to adulthood. Later, with imaginations having been fuelled by the choicest supernatural stories of werewolves and their variant local forms, it is no wonder that the wolf became such an object of hatred that it was virtually eliminated in many areas of the world where it used to be found. Not helping its cause was the confounding fact that it was a predator that often came into conflict with man by lifting poultry and livestock during harsh climatic times of prey scarcity.

In India, the wolf (*Canis lupus*) is an endangered species listed in Schedule 1 of the Wildlife (Protection) Act. It is surely a debatable issue whether the decline in its population was the result of sustained elimination, or due to the loss of its habitat to the ever-burgeoning agricultural activity in the country. But chances are that it was a combination of both these factors that pushed the wolf into the endangered category. The increase in agriculture activity must have manifested in decreasing wolf habitats and falling population levels, while the other effect would have been an increase in man-wolf conflicts, resulting in further downsizing of wolf populations due to elimination of aberrant packs.

However, the wolf seems to have made an appearance in the state. The recent report of child-killing by a wolf in a village near Rae Bareli is disturbing in the sense that it brings to mind a spate of similar incidents that happened in eastern Uttar Pradesh during 1996-97 when many children were injured or killed in wolf attacks. One also remembers that the childhood fear lurking in the subconscious minds and imaginations of the simple village folk affected by those incidents, gave rise to so many illusionary villains like the 'manhai', a man who transformed into a wolf in order to satiate his desire to eat a succulent child.

The media fallout of those events was instrumental in wildlife scientists and forest officials making an in-depth study of the problem. Dr YV Jhala, faculty member of the Wildlife Institute of India and an expert on wolves, conducted a research in the affected areas during March to October 1996, in order to ascertain the identity of the predator responsible for these attacks, as well as to determine the causes for this aberrant behaviour, in case it was indeed wolves that were to be blamed.

During the course of the study, about 70 cases of attacks causing injury and death to children were taken into account. Sites of attacks, remains of killed children, autopsy reports and the evidences like hair and pugmarks left by the predator were examined. Data pertaining to location, date and time of attacks were analysed to determine the area of operation and their chorological trend. The availability of both wild and domestic prey-base in the area of study was used as an indicator to assess the levels to which children of that area could become the target of wolf predation.

The study inferred that it was indeed a single wolf that was responsible for the attacks, the frequency of attack being one in three days, while the average rate of the victim being killed was once every five days. The reason why children were targeted was that most of them ranged between the ages of 4 months to 9 years, and were more vulnerable as compared to village livestock. Moreover, there was also clear indication of some form of neglect by the parents, which caused the children becoming easy targets.

Therefore, in view of the present case of the reported wolf attack, it would be a good idea to take a lesson from the past, and focus on creating awareness among the affected populace, so that they do not put down their guard, or become victims of wild rumours once again. Moreover, with the present Chief Wildlife Warden himself having being an active field campaigner when the previous wolf attacks occurred, it can safely be assumed that the Forest Department would have no problems in taking full control over the man-wolf conflict that has presented itself today.

LIFTING OF US SANCTIONS MAY BOOST WILDLIFE CONSERVATION IN INDIA

September 25, 2001

Notwithstanding the immense human tragedy witnessed in the collapse of the WTC towers, it can be said that the speedy global realignments that occurred in its aftermath, were directly responsible for creating the political expediency that steered US President Bush's decision of lifting economic sanctions against both India and Pakistan.

Speaking strictly from the point of view of wildlife conservation in India, this news may be cause for elation, since it broadens the prospect of increased US funding to state forest departments and Indian NGO's that are actively involved in conservation projects related to the highly endangered species like the Indian tiger (*Panthera tigris*), the one-horned rhino (*Rhinoceros unicornis*) and the Asian elephant (*Elephas maximus*).

It may be recalled that the United States had taken the decision of imposing economic sanctions on India immediately after the nuclear tests in May 1998. Amongst many other financial assistance programmes that came under the purview of these sanctions, was the termination or suspension of US assistance to India for conservation projects related to the tiger and rhino under its Rhinoceros and Tiger Conservation Act of 1994.

This Act is specifically aimed at providing financial resources for the conservation programs of various nations whose activities affect global rhinoceros and tiger populations. It was promulgated by the US Government in view of the fact that rhino and tiger populations throughout the world were under extreme threat of extinction, despite their being listed on Appendix I of the Convention on International Trade in Endangered Species of Wild Fauna and Flora (CITES).

Constituted under this Act, the purpose of the Rhinoceros and Tiger Conservation Fund is to augment the rhinoceros and tiger conservation by providing financial assistance to projects that are primarily aimed at habitat / ecosystem management, protected area / reserve management, enforcement of wildlife law, development of forensic skills, and achievement of sustainable development in buffer zones of tiger / rhinoceros habitats.

Considering that India still has a fair share of the population of both these species in its national parks and tiger reserves, US assistance was being provided to a number of state forest departments and other wildlife conservation agencies in the form of grants routed through the federal US Fish & Wildlife Service.

But, as a result of these sanctions coming into effect, financial assistance to India under the Rhinoceros and Tiger Conservation Fund did suffer a temporary setback. Funding of ongoing projects had to be put on hold, while new project proposals submitted to the US Fish and Wildlife Service were stalled during the period during which the sanctions were in place.

Thankfully however, this period of uncertainty did not last long. In October 1999, an Amendment passed by the US Senate provided waiver authority to President Clinton to suspend some of the sanctions against both India and Pakistan. Using the powers vested in him through this Amendment, President Clinton indefinitely waived a number of economic sanctions against both countries, but what was heartening from the point of view of wildlife conservation in India, was the fact that it also included the restoration of financial assistance to the Rhinoceros and Tiger Conservation Fund, as well as to the Asian Elephant Conservation Fund.

During the past five years, the US Fish and Wildlife Service has been instrumental in providing financial assistance to 19 projects involving tiger and rhino conservation in India. Additionally, it has also invited project proposals of up to 30,000 dollars each, to be funded during the current fiscal year. This is probably just the kind of opportunity required by the state forest departments and conservation NGO's to take advantage of this offer and prepare project proposals that augment the financial resources for their on-going conservation activities in various protected areas across the country

MIGRATORY WATERFOWL LIKELY TO BE HIT BY WAR IN AFGHANISTAN

October 10, 2001

At long last, the inevitable military strikes by US-led coalition are now pounding Afghanistan with the avowed intention of neutralising the much-touted enemy. Curiously though, striking a strange note of harmony with the rhetorical justifications for the first war of the twenty-first century, are a great number of sympathetic voices too, including those of the coalition, who mouth strong words of concern for the safety and well-being of the hapless civilian population of the country, which has so unfortunately been caught up in the vortex of this 'crime and punishment' game.

In a sense, it is a history of sorts being made when we witness the unique combination of two different types of payloads being air-dropped on Afghanistan – deadly bombs and accurate tomahawks that blaze a fiery trail of destruction during the night, while relief and succour comes to the bedraggled lot during the day in the form of rations and medicines. Being fortified with such a well-conceived humanitarian icing, it is quite possible that the inherent ravages of this war might fail to prick the collective conscience of a lot of peace-loving people, as far as human suffering is concerned.

But I wonder whether the non-human subject of my concern is tenable enough to be even mentioned at such a time. The month of October is the time when a lot of migratory waterfowl would be present in Afghanistan, temporarily inhabiting the lakes and wetlands there, before undertaking the final leg of their southward journey to better climes in India. Given the present state of turmoil that exists there, it is obvious that the fate of migratory waterfowl is bound to be of least priority in Afghanistan at the moment, and it can only be speculated as to what adverse effects the war is likely to have on these species, once their habitat areas get caught in the cross-fire.

One does not have to be a military strategist to presume that after the initial salvo of missiles is directed at the cities to neutralise the administrative and military assets of the retreating Taliban, the next phase of action is likely to be spread out over remote areas of the country, where the intended targets will supposedly take refuge. This will be the time for real concern for the birds, since some of Afghanistan's prime wetlands are bound to be located in these remote areas. Once military action starts in these areas, it would cause extensive disturbance to the resident and migratory waterfowl which would be either wintering, or staging in the lakes such as Ab-e-Istada & Dashte Nawar in Ghazni province, and Kole Hashmat Khan near Kabul.

According to past studies, the wetland ecosystem of Afghanistan is created by its rivers that have no natural outlet to the sea, and hence they drain into a series of depressions, which form large shallow saline lakes and marshes. The beds of these wetlands are constituted of the sediments transported by the rivers, which makes them the most biologically productive ecosystems in the country, and therefore constitute viable waterfowl habitats.

Of the seven wetlands in Afghanistan, the three considered by ornithologists as being of international importance for migrating and wintering waterfowls are Ab-e-Istada and Dashte Nawar which are important habitats for migrating or wintering waders and ducks. They also support large breeding colonies of greater flamingos (*Phoenicopterus ruber*). In addition, Ab-e-Istada also has the distinction of being regularly visited by the entire migrating populations of the highly endangered Siberian crane (*Grus leucogeranus*). The third important wetland is the Kole Hashmat Khan on the outskirts of Kabul, which is also supposed to be rich in bird biodiversity, hosting a large number of ducks and coots during winters.

As things stand today, I believe that there can be no doubting the presumption that the high-powered strikes being currently launched in and around these areas, are sure to be potent enough to destabilize the birds, as they go about their natural business of wintering or staging in the lakes as part of their natural migratory pattern.

However, notwithstanding the fact that Afghanistan has been consistently ravaged by war during the past 20 years or so, one can but fervently hope that during all these years the birds have found ways and means to circumvent the adversity brought upon them by the never-ending follies of man.

MAN-ELEPHANT CONFLICT TAKES HEAVY TOLL

October 31, 2001

While writing last week, I had mentioned that one of the unconfirmed causes for the death of seven elephants in Assam's Nameri national park during the month of August, had been attributed to anthrax infection. I had also rued the fact that a lack of a proper follow-up on the media report published in the Assam Tribune was the reason why this suspicion of anthrax being the possible contaminant, could not be confirmed at the time of writing.

In a bid to remedy this self-deprecation, as well as to clarify logical queries that may have been raised in the minds of readers, I tried to acquire some additional information on this issue. But to my utmost chagrin, I now find that the malady was in fact far greater than was reported, and that the death of the seven elephants was only the tip of a deadly iceberg, with the actual number of elephants succumbing exceeding more than thirty.

According to information provided by Guwahati based Manju Barua, an active conservationist and a member of the Standing Committee of Indian Board for Wildlife, there is grave concern for the wild elephants of Assam, since it is evident that a sort of 'silent war' has been declared against them by some people within one single district of Sonitpur. It is staggering to know that in a matter of about 70 days during

July to September this year, 31 elephants have been poisoned to death there.

It all started with the death of 20 elephants, which were poisoned in and around Nameri National Park and Naduar RF in Sonitpur East Division between July 3rd and 13th August. However, in spite of clear indications that this mass death of elephants could be due to poisoning, the forest department reportedly failed to activate the Police machinery to identify and apprehend the culprits who perpetrated the crime. As a result, the perpetrators were presumably encouraged to carry on this mode of extermination and subsequently, in the next month (Aug-Sept 2001), 4 more elephants were poisoned in Charduar RF, Dhekiajuli. This was followed by another carnage with 7 elephants being poisoned to death near Tezpur airport in Goroimari, which incidentally was a Reserve Forest before the airport was established.

The root cause of this tragedy lies in the ever-increasing man-animal conflict that percolates to almost all parts of the country where forests and wildlife are located. And as always happens, it is the wildlife that ends up paying the heaviest toll. In the present case, Barua contends that it had been long evident that this area was vulnerable enough to precipitate such a `silent cleansing' of the elephant population. The three primary indicators to this effect were (a) a systematic destruction of elephant habitat in the district, (b) the local people's protests against elephant-depredation progressively taking a more organized form, and (c) the fact that various experts had been in agreement about identifying this district as a representative area for elephant depredation.

In order to analyse the level of man-elephant conflict that catalysed this fatal and revengeful act, Barua outlines that the five reserve forests (RF) located in the eastern part of the district where these mass killings are occurring, have experienced systematic destruction of forests for the purpose of agriculture and homestead. A forest department survey conducted in 1999 enumerates that the area under encroachment in most of these RF's ranged from 40 to 70 percent. Most of these encroached areas are now agricultural fields, which the locals cultivate for paddy and other crop. Wild elephants that perforce intrude into these areas because of their own shrinking habitat, are regarded as pests and dealt with as such, with gruesome consequences.

But now that the deadly deed has been committed, the least that should be done by authorities - apart from catching the culprits - is to take appropriate action in tackling the root causes of the crisis. It should be logically inferred that if whole communities in these areas are turning hostile, there has to be a genuine reason that needs to be tackled in its entirety rather than it being dealt with in a superficial manner. This would necessarily encompass measures to reduce crop depredations, dealing with the complex issue of illegal encroachments, and adequately compensating farmers for the losses they are incurring. Unless this is done, mere apprehensions of poachers / killers is not likely to redress the problem of man-animal conflict in any part of the country.

ANTHRAX AS A POTENT WILDLIFE KILLER

October 24, 2001

In the backdrop of the current frenzy being generated by anthrax amongst fear-crazed humans in some parts of the world, it may be a good opportunity to spare a thought for the threats that are posed by anthrax on many vulnerable wildlife species.

Anthrax is basically an animal disease that has a long-recorded history, which means that it has been occurring in domestic cattle for hundreds of years. During all this time, it has not been credited with causing any serious disease of epidemic proportions in humans, although stray cases of infections have always been reported from amongst people working closely with cattle or sheep.

It is caused by the bacterium *Bacillus anthracis* that regenerates itself through the formation of long-lasting spores. These spores have the inherent capability of dormancy, which enables them to survive for a long time in the environment. Grass-eating animals, including wild herbivores, are prone to infection because they are more likely to ingest anthrax spores living in the soil. Although the remedial practice of animal vaccination, or in case of an outbreak, the destruction of infected herds, has been instrumental in checking the disease, anthrax spores still continue to be found in soil samples from all over the world.

In far as wild species are concerned, all mammals are susceptible to infection, but as stated earlier, it is the herbivores and grazers that are more vulnerable. Once the

53

anthrax infection is established in herbivores, it ultimately causes death, with the carcasses exuding dark tarry blood from body orifices. Unless quickly found and disposed off by burning, these carcasses are fed upon by wild scavengers like the hyaenas and jackals, and thereby the spores are spread across to other places, including waterholes. The spread of contamination is further augmented by flies and other insects that feed on the carcasses, and transfer the spores to surrounding vegetation.

As has been documented in a recently televised film on African wildlife, an outbreak of anthrax in Kruger national park – if memory serves one right - also caused lions to become infected after they had fed on anthrax carcasses. It was heartrending to see large prides of infected lions, with grotesque and swollen faces, slowly but surely dying even after all the ministrations of the committed park staff. However, the subsequent operation they launched in disposing off the carcasses by burning, and disinfecting large areas around where the outbreak had occurred, gave a graphic insight into the huge human and logistic effort that wildlife managers in that country are capable of mounting.

In India however, our forests and wildlife have either not been afflicted with any anthrax epidemic of notable proportions, or have not identified it as the cause in cases where wildlife has been reported to die in substantial numbers. The most recent scare of a possible anthrax outbreak in an Indian forest that comes to mind, is the report in the Assam Tribune of August 15, 2001, which mentioned the death of seven wild elephants in the Nameri national park. According to the report, the Sonitpur district veterinary department suspected that the unnatural deaths of the wild tuskers could be due to anthrax, which had reportedly spread in an epidemic form in the nearby forests of Arunachala Pradesh.

Unfortunately, a lack of a follow up on that report has not provided any confirmation whether it was indeed anthrax or not. But what one does hope is that such an outbreak does not touch our forests and wildlife because it would be very presumptuous and optimistic to hope for such remedial operations in India, as were mounted in that national park in Africa.

DEMOISELLE CRANES FLY SAFELY INTO INDIA

November 7, 2001

Without any intention of pushing too far a point that has already been made in this column earlier (October 10th), I sincerely hope that it might still be considered judicious by readers if I were to take recourse to a follow-up on the fears that were expressed therein, about the safety of migratory birds, as they traversed through their war-confounded habitat in Afghanistan, and flew into safer climes in India.

Although fearing the worst for the birds in the war-zone, as they went about their natural migratory pattern of staging or wintering in the lakes of Afghanistan, I had nevertheless voiced a strong sense of optimism that their natural instincts would definitely teach them ways to circumvent the adversity brought upon them by the current turmoil.

On that point, there seems to be good news at hand. Ornithologists and amateur birdwatchers who have been keeping a close watch on the arrival of the migrating birds, have reported that despite the deafening sounds of aircraft and explosion of bombs on the flight path over Afghanistan, a great number of Demoiselle cranes have made their way into one their favourite places, the tiny village of Keechan, near the township of Phalodi in Rajasthan. This village lies at a peaceful location about 4 km inside from the main highway, and is equidistant from Bikaner, Jodhpur and Jaisalmer.

According to N. Shivakumar, an ornithologist who extensively toured the area recently, about 4000 cranes have arrived at Keechan by now, although their number is likely to swell to about 10,000 as newer arrivals make their way to rest and roost there for the winters. The reason why these demoiselles have consistently shown a marked preference for Keechan as a wintering area, lies in the fact that the villagers go to great lengths for providing ample safety and food to these winged visitors flying in from distant countries.

Nearly 500 kg of grain per day, paid for by donations from local people and keen visitors, is laid out for the birds. Two small organizations operated by the locals, are reportedly performing an efficient conservation that is almost akin to what the Vishnois are doing for the blackbuck. So protective are the villagers about the birds that they resent any intrusion by unruly tourists, although they happily allow birdwatchers and ornithologists free and unhindered access to the place.

Like any other committed wildlifer, Shivakumar surmises that there can be but two ways of looking at the present disturbed situation in Afghanistan. Either the number of demoiselle cranes coming to India could swell if they abandon their usual stops in Afghanistan and Pakistan, or else many would perish while attempting to fly to their respective wintering grounds.

As far as the actual ground situation in Afghanistan is concerned, Sudhir Vyas, an Indian official posted in Pakistan, and an avid birdwatcher, says that there is no specific information on what effect the bombing in Afghanistan has had, or may have on cranes migrating over that country.

But it would be worth considering that common cranes seem to enter Pakistan from Afghanistan along two major routes (i) the bulk from just under the Safed Koh range south of the Khyber, and then in a concentrated movement along the Kurram River valley till its junction with the Indus; and (ii) the rest over Quetta and areas immediately south of it, over the Afghanistan-Baluchistan border. The demoiselles also follow the same main routes but over a broader front. Some also enter from the north, over the Pamirs, then down into the Punjab through the Gilgit and Hunza valleys.

Vyas speculates that this last northern route would appear to be largely unaffected by the situation in Afghanistan. But birds coming in through the first route would have to cross the Hindu Kush ranges somewhere southwest of Kabul, and those taking the second route would presumably come around the Hindu Kush over Herat and then over the Kandahar desert. Both routes cross the main areas where the bombings are going on, and there would certainly be heavy disturbance.

However, there is one small ray of hope. If for some reason – either military or diplomatic - the bombings were to be discontinued for even a month during ramazan, it could give just a few days of peace to the demoiselle cranes, the common cranes as well as to the Siberian cranes, to come safely into our country.

UP WETLANDS MAY PROVIDE IMPROVED HABITATS TO MIGRATORY WATERFOWL IN FUTURE

October 17, 2001

There was a time - not so long ago, it seems – when the onset of winter brought in its wake a great annual event, that of flock after flock of migrating ducks and geese flying overhead. Those of us who have been interested witnesses to this unique phenomenon will never fail to remember the feeling of happiness evoked by the sight of the V-formation of greylag and bar-headed geese flying languorously on moonlit nights, and the intermittent sounds of their raucous honking wafting down as they passed overhead. Interspersed with their passage were the flocks of other waterfowl like the teals, pintails, pochards and mallards, whose flights seemed to be more frantic, as though they were in a hurry to reach their destination before it was too late.

Those were happy times, when nights were not spent in the claustrophobic confines of modern bedrooms, but sleeping out in the open verandahs and courtyards of sprawling homes, which gave us the opportunity of watching these migratory birds being urged on strongly by their deep homing instinct.

Today, rapid urbanisation and changed lifestyles may not give us the pleasure of sighting these migratory waterfowl in flight, but they still arrive as they did in the past, to spend the winters in the lakes and *jheels* spread across the country. It is these wetlands that are their temporary homes for the birds, as they fly into India from the northern countries to escape the harsh and snowy winters there.

Apart from being important for the migratory waterfowl, the importance of wetlands lies in the fact that they are highly productive ecosystems not only for the migrants but also for endemic species of fauna and flora that are dependent on them all year round. They constitute a natural system for regulating monsoon run-offs by absorbing water and therefore reducing flood risks. The presence of water and essential nutrients in wetlands makes them a dynamic source of life to a huge bio-diversity that exists within them.

Considering the importance of wetlands, both government agencies and conservation organizations are undertaking various projects for their conservation. One such ongoing joint project of the Ministry of Environment & Forests and UNDP has been awarded to the Coimbatore based Salim Ali Centre for Ornithology & Natural History (SACON). This project is aimed at identification, conservation and enhancing sustainable use of globally significant wetlands of India, including those in Uttar Pradesh.

Under this project, more than 700 wetlands of over 2.25 hectares in size, will be surveyed and mapped, and then prioritized on the basis of their water quality and biodiversity values - mainly waterfowl, aquatic vegetation and fish. Based on that priority, conservation measures will be launched to enhance their quality and sustainability for the biodiversity dependent on them.

Since the state of Uttar Pradesh is also richly endowed with a number of wetlands spread uniformly over all the districts, this project will go a long way in improving the sustainability of about 30 to 50 wetlands which are expected to qualify for selection.

It is understandable that such a project is of a large magnitude and therefore would require enormous manpower and inter-institutional collaboration. In order to fulfill this requirement, SACON has invited the participation of large number of institutions and individuals from all over India. State-level coordinators have been identified for each state, and have been entrusted the work of coordinating field studies in their respective states.

For Uttar Pradesh and Uttaranchal, this assignment will be conducted by Dr Arun Kumar, Joint Director of the Zoological Survey of India, Dehradun. He proposes to hold a one-day workshop at Dehradun in November, in order to identify a set of 30-50 wetlands, as well as institutions and individuals to carry out field studies during December 2001 and January 2002. The field study would be for a period of 3 days, to be held simultaneously at each wetland, and involve the collection of data on pre-determined parameters.

It would be a good opportunity for enthusiastic individuals from across the state to contribute to the success of this project. Maybe sometime in the future, their contribution would help in improving the habitat of migratory waterfowl in the state, and earn them gratitude from the birds.

HOW LONG-LASTING ARE CONSERVATION VICTORIES?

November 11, 2001

When one considers the large number of NGO's and individuals who are ostensibly engaged in the wildlife conservation movement in India, it should be both logical and safe for one to assume that, either singularly or collectively, they would surely be achieving major victories in their ongoing battle against the combination of powerful commercial interests like mining, timber extraction, tourism and transport etc, which seem all too eager to rip through whatever little is still left of our wilderness.

Unfortunately, most of the feedback coming from the field seems to indicate that this is not so. With regular reports of destruction of wildlife at the hands of poachers, and denudation of forests by large-scale infrastructure development projects, it is increasingly becoming clear that the most frustrating aspects which the proponents of the conservation movement have to contend with, is the lack of any worthwhile victories – victories that are not just temporary, but which could withstand the passage of time, and still be tangible enough to be savoured as success.

It is probably a combination of two of the most clichéd reasons that is responsible for this state of affairs. Firstly, our country continues to have an uncontrolled population, which has bourgeoned out of all proportions even near and around the Protected Areas (PA's), thereby bringing a huge pressure to bear upon the natural resources therein. Secondly, lured by profit, commercial projects like mining, timber, tourism and transport consistently make a beeline for these areas, and are equally responsible for creating destructive inroads into PA's.

The conservation organisations try to battle it out with these government or corporate bodies in courts of law. They sometimes do achieve euphoric victories, like the ones achieved in Corbett national park where a proposed highway through its southern periphery was halted, or the one in Bihar, where local activists secured realignment of a proposed railway line from Hazaribagh to Koderma so that it did not pass through the Hazaribagh National Park. But it is another matter however, that subsequent reversal of rulings, amendments in law, or simply non-execution of judicial orders, takes the sheen away soon enough, veritably turning these temporary victories into permanent defeats.

In order to outline how ephemeral these conservation victories can prove to be with the passage of time, it may be pertinent to recall that in 1999, the Wildlife Protection Society of India (WPSI), a Delhi-based conservation organisation had sought intervention in an ongoing legal case between the state Irrigation and the Forest department, and had been able to secure a favourable order from the Lucknow High Court on the basis of the wildlife conservation issue raised in its intervention petition.

The judicial conflict involved the non-return of about 802.3 hectares of land belonging to the Corbett National Park (CNP) by the Irrigation department, which it was under agreement to do, subsequent to the completion of the Kalagarh dam on the Ramganga river within CNP.

Although the Irrigation Department completed work on the dam in 1971, the land in excess of its requirement for maintenance and upkeep of the dam was not transferred back to the forest department. Gradually this chunk of land was reportedly colonised illegally by people who had nothing to do with the Irrigation department. Based on research it had conducted, the WPSI apprised the court that this bustling human colony was responsible for blocking the principal migratory route of the westernmost population of Asian elephants, between Corbett and Rajaji national parks.

Taking cognizance of this contention, the appropriate directives were issued by the court so as to facilitate the removal of the colony and restoration of this migration corridor to the wild elephants. But where human beings are concerned, human rights can't be far behind. Quick on the uptake, the adversaries of these orders brought into play the argument that ejecting the residents would be against their basic human rights, as well as against natural justice. Since then, this has been the convenient smokescreen that has prevented the authorities from executing the court orders.

This is definitely not to aver that human rights are less paramount in comparison to those of wildlife, but one only wishes that those espousing the cause of human rights should also be aware that there is an equally vital need for wildlife conservation too. It is for them to realise that wildlife itself looks towards humans to manage it, and thereby is deserving of their sympathy in making concessions that contribute to its survival in whatever few areas that still remain.

It is for the amalgamation of this essential ingredient in our characters that the knowledge of ecological principles, and the concepts of ecological fragility, should be strictly made part of learning for our present and future generations.

FAKE TIGER SKINS: A KNOTTY DISGUISE

Dec 5, 2001

Last week, wildlife enthusiasts may have been perturbed by two media reports pertaining to the seizure of eight tiger skins from different parts of the country. The first one reported the recovery of six full-length tiger skins in Kolkata on Sunday. Two days later, this was followed by news from closer home, that two persons in possession of two tiger skins and one leopard skin, were arrested on Tuesday near Noida, in UP.

It goes without saying that both these reports would have caused a huge amount of distress to conservation-minded readers, since it evidently was a pointer to the fact that another eight tigers, from out of the precarious wild population that remains in the country, had been done to death by poachers to supply the illegal demand for tiger skin and bones.

If it can be of any consolation for such readers, it may be informed that subsequent examination of these skins by experts has clarified that all the 'tiger' skins were in fact fakes, crafted out of the skin of other animals, and painted to resemble the real thing. However, adding a sinister dimension to an otherwise harmless-seeming trade in fake skins, was the disconcerting revelation that the leopard skin was a genuine article.

Which obviously bring us to the question of the extent of the illegal trade in tiger skins and bones, and why the seizure of fake tiger skins, and the arrest of persons dealing in them, is as much a matter for concern as the trade in the real thing.

It is common knowledge that the illegal wildlife trade is an international one. According to Interpol, the business is worth an estimated $6 billion a year, second only to illegal trade in narcotics. As far as the component of tiger derivatives is concerned, the supply comes mainly through poaching, which is taking place in almost all tiger range countries where the species is still found in the wild. But wherever the tiger poaching may have occurred, its parts are nonetheless headed towards one single major destination, where they are put to end-use as ingredients for Traditional Chinese Medicine (TCM).

And if anyone were to imagine that the use or manufacture of TCM would only be restricted to China, he would be wrong. It is a matter of grave concern for naturalists that in spite of all the restrictions imposed within different countries by local legislations, or through international treaties like the Convention on International Trade in Endangered Species of Wild Fauna and Flora (CITES), almost all the developed countries in the world continue to have a market for TCM containing tiger ingredients, and it is thriving illegally with the support of the unholy alliance between the manufacturers and the users.

This enterprise is thriving because there is no end to the number of humans for whom the tiger is a just a symbol of strength and virility, and they would go to any length to attain its prowess. So you would have any number of ageing Don Juans the world over, desperately seeking a bowl of tiger penis soup in a bid to fortify their sagging libido. Further, the myth of the magical healing powers of tiger parts, creates a huge demand for medicines for ailments as far ranging as acute ones like arthritis, rheumatism or skin diseases, to such mundane – but irritating nonetheless – ones like bad breath.

It is probably these patients who are the real villains, actually responsible for creating the demand for TCM, and thereby bringing the tiger to such a plight. As long as this demand is kept up, tigers would continue to be poached wherever they are still found. Although it may sound simplistic, there is surely some weight in the logic that the killing would stop only when the buying stops.

By the same token, the escalating trade in fake tiger skins is also very worrying, since it is a response indicative of the demand and supply phenomenon. It is because of the perceived demand in the illegal market for tiger derivatives, that fakes are generated. Even as a smart marketing strategy, the successful transaction of even one fake tiger skin would give the trader that much more leverage for dishing out other fake derivatives like bones, claws, nails, fat etc, all ostensibly coming from the same individual 'tiger'.

However, linked to this fake trade in India, is another gloomy question that comes to mind. Could it be that genuine tiger skins are now too hard to come by - not as much due to impeccable protection and enforcement, but simply because there are hardly any tigers left in the wild? Perish the thought.

WHO CARES FOR THE WILD HERE ANYWAY?

Dec 12, 2001

Hardly a week passes without the emanation of some distressing news that spells huge setbacks for wildlife conservation in the country. The regularity with which wildlife is being assailed by forces inimical to it, and the stark failure of agencies established to manage and protect it, makes it all the more traumatic.

This time the scene shifts to neighbouring Uttaranchal where two unconnected incidents give us reason to believe that the dismal track record of wildlife and forest conservation, which the nascent state has generated till date, is surely not on the upswing.

The incident that needs first mention is the killing of two male elephants in the Rajaji national park two days ago. As it happened in Corbett national park during the culmination of last year and the early months of this one, poachers have been successful in intruding into the Rajaji national park and killing the elephants for their tusks. According to reports, this time the poachers did not resort to the gun, but used poison instead, to kill these tuskers near the Kunao forest range, close to the town of Rishikesh.

As usually happens in the aftermath of any disaster or crime, this incident too will be followed by routine motions like combing operations by a motley posse of security forces and forest guards, unconvincing sound bytes from people in the 'know', and a temporary 'upping' of the guard all around the state, before fleeting memory brings on relaxation to us, and respite to the poacher before he strikes again at our amnesia.

The other incident that has the future potential of delivering a deathly blow to Corbett Tiger Reserve, is the introduction of a public bus service between Kalagarh and Ramnagar via Jhirna, on the forest road lying in the southern boundary of the reserve. For starters, this bus has been assigned a single return trip on the 40-odd kilometre route, but the matter for concern lies in the fact that this road had been closed to public transport since it was taken over by the forest department subsequent to the relocation of villages at Jhirna and Kothi Rau in the early '90s. As a result, this area has seen a rapid return to wilderness, with tigers and elephants regularly frequenting it on their beat.

The extent of disturbance that public transport would bring in its wake for the wildlife of that area is positively going to border on the extreme. However, what is again a painful reminder of our own amnesia, is that it was only April this year when the Supreme Court had taken note of the tree felling on this proposed Kotdwar-Kalagarh-Ramnagar highway, and ordered restraint on further such activity. That order had been passed by the Court after it had been made to understand that this activity would be a long-time detriment for the Corbett Tiger Reserve, and the wildlife it contained.

Although that order was celebrated by all of us as a definite victory for wildlife conservation, but with the introduction of this bus service, it now seems that we'll live to see that advantage frittering away, as this highway comes into being. To the credit or discredit of the planners, it may be conceded that this route alignment is unfortunately much too direct and short for the Uttaranchal government to give it up - Corbett or no Corbett. What must have determined the ultimate decision in this issue was probably their contention that use of this route is ideally aligned to save Uttaranchal transporters and passengers from a longer circuit, and also pre-empts their use (and consequent tax liability) of the existing Uttar Pradesh roads between Kalagarh and Ramnagar. It is virtually established that if this issue of taxation were to be resolved, the need for using this forest road could have been kept on the back-burner, where it actually belongs.

And so does the cookie crumble for the wildlife of Uttaranchal. How unfortunate that it has to contend with silly, man-made boundaries between the states of the country, which render us so far apart.

DRAINING OF WETLANDS BECOMES POINT OF CONTENTION

January 9, 2002

It was in June last year, that the very first issue raised in this column was the proposed draining of wetlands located in the Etawah and Mainpuri districts, as part of an agricultural developmental project primarily aimed at boosting productivity. All very well, except for the fact that these wetlands happened to be a prime habitat that supported substantial populations of large avian species like the Sarus and the Black-necked Stork, as well as other aquatic fauna and flora.

According to warnings sounded at that time by environmentalists and wildlife researchers connected with this area, the devastation of these wetlands had the potential of posing a serious threat to the survival of many of these life forms, even to the extent of obliterating some species that did not have the capacity to move away to other habitats.

Six months later, the issue apparently seems to be unresolved. One does not doubt that the authorities have taken serious note of the opinion of conservationists, and one also concedes there must have been strong compulsions for the implementation of the project to go on.

Be that as it may, I have received one frantic SOS, which has been circulated just today by Harsh Vardhan, a concerned bird lover from Jaipur. It is a high-pitched, fervent appeal from someone who is obviously distressed by what is happening in an area that is considered sacrosanct from the point of view of wildlife conservation. Due to a time constraint, I am unfortunately not in a position to verify many of the points raised by Harsh Vardhan, but would nevertheless like to share his concern with readers who may have some interest in this issue.

Following is a version of the text of the appeal, which has been abridged for the purpose of brevity, as well as to shear it of the element of seeming rhetoric that tends to creep into such communiques. "The Wetlands of Mainpuri and Etawah are being sold to private people. For agricultural purposes, they are being drained out. The priority is to honour a World Bank assisted project in India's Uttar Pradesh. Obviously, the project meant to be scrapped in favour of aquatic ecological gains to people, is now put on top gear.

"It is happening in Mainpuri and Etawah districts of Uttar Pradesh. The bulldozers have been rolled down the edges of the wetlands to implement the World Bank project. Against the bulldozers stands a tiny paper, an order issued by the District Magistrates of Mainpuri and Etawah which opposes the move to drain off the wetlands.

"The District Magistrates say 'no' to draining process, for they know the needs of people. It looks like a piece of positive good news that the two District Magistrates have realised (the) significance of maintaining wetlands. Mr. Naresh Kumar, District Magistrate and Collector of Mainpuri, and Mr. S.P. Goyal, District Magistrate and Collector of Etawah, deserve congratulations. Well done, the Indian community needs more such young IAS decision makers.

"Mr. R.L. Singh, Chief Wildlife Warden of Uttar Pradesh, has already issued necessary orders to support the large wetlands in these two districts in order to ensure sustainable conditions for the Indian Sarus Cranes, Black-necked Storks and other avifauna supported therein. He has a viable proposal to develop a Sanctuary for Indian Sarus Cranes in one of the wetlands facing threat from draining.

"Who will succeed? As things stand on 7 January 2002 in these northern Indo-Gangetic plains of India, the wetlands are in danger of losing their water within few weeks! So, people should be ready to face colossal loss of aquatic ecology, birds, animals and the consequent benefits to agricultural practices and life system for the rural communities. It will be a long-term loss in face of short-term gains. The gainers shall be few. Losers will be many, and for a long time.

"Dear citizens, can you do something? BC Chaudhary, Principal Scientist stationed at Wildlife Institute of India, Dehradun, today needs your help. Gopi Sundar, working at Etawah for WII, appeals to you to stand in favour of wetlands. Rise up folks. It is time to act".

A TRIBUTE TO CHARGER – THE LONG LIVING TIGER

January 2, 2002

There have been quite a number of wild tigers that have become famous during their lifetime, by virtue of either some special characteristic inherent in them, or due to the mere fact that their high visibility in the forest has been instrumental in making them subjects of sustained documentation of their lives through extensive photographs and text.

The ones that come readily to mind are Sheroo, the Corbett tiger that attained fame initially due to his easy demeanour and high visibility, but later became infamous after his mauling of Subedar Ali, a forest department staffer posted in Corbett. Then there was Dhitoo, another robust male tiger from Corbett, whose infamy condemned him to an existence in the Kanpur Zoo after he mauled and killed David Hunt, an English birdwatcher on a visit to the tiger reserve. In Bandhavgarh tiger reserve, there was the legendary tigress Sita, who attained international recognition for her high fecundity and the large number of litters that she bore during her lifetime.

But very few wild tigers have been able to achieve a reputation as awesome as the one that has gone the way of a male tiger called Charger, who was till recently a resident of Bandhavgarh national park in Madhya Pradesh, located about 250 kms south of Allahabad. For almost the entire decade of the nineties, Charger happened to be the most feared and talked about tiger, for both the tourists as well as the wildlife managers of Bandhavgarh.

As his name suggests, Charger was so called because of his instinctive propensity to charge at vehicles and riding elephants that tended to come too close for his comfort. Since tiger behaviour can vary extremely with different individuals, this inherent characteristic of Charger was acknowledged and respected by all, once he established his territory on the tourism zone in Bandhavgarh.

Fortunately, Charger was able to continue holding his territory for almost ten years, and sired many litters till he died naturally last year of old age and consequent debility. During his last days he did run into trouble, unable to hunt after being injured and chased away from his territory by a young dominant male, but that was all a part of the natural sequence that wild tigers go through. What was of importance was the fact that Charger had been able to live naturally as long as wild tigers are supposed to do, and his passing away left no regrets.

Charger's life and times have now been documented in the form of a book titled 'Charger – the long living tiger'. It has been authored by Shahbaz Ahmed, a 1981 batch IFS officer of MP cadre, who was Field Director of Bandhavgarh tiger reserve at the time of Charger's death, and has been published by Print World, an Allahabad based publishing house. The book contains text that delves into the realm of tiger behaviour from a writer who possesses a deep insight of the subject, and it is also beautifully embellished with photographs of Charger. It carries a graphic account of the last days of Charger, when he had to be rescued from certain starvation, and possible poaching, after he was chased away from his territory and spotted in the buffer zone of the reserve. There are also interesting accounts of actual encounters which people had with Charger, and the viciousness which he was able to convey during all the mock charges that he made at his terrified targets, although he never as much as hurt any human being during his entire life.

Which brings me to my own encounter with Charger – an entirely insipid affair. It was in 1993 during my first visit to the park, which was around the same time that Charger had just begun to make his reputation. The forest guide in my Gypsy had most emphatically made us turn away, to prevent approaching a huge male tiger that sat in a bamboo thicket bordering the grassland. In answer to my protest, the guide explained that this particular tiger was very dangerous, liable to charge us on further approach. He said it was called PP Singh. Well, I accepted. Maybe it was named after some tough Field Director who had at one time been the scourge of the staff. No, I was informed. They called him so because he had once charged so viciously at an elephant carrying some tourists that one of the terrified riders had lost control of his sphincter muscles, and let go on the elephant.

It was then that the penny dropped! Before he became famous as Charger, he was known as *pee pee* Singh.

INDIAN BOARD FOR WILDLIFE MEETS AFTER A FIVE-YEAR GAP

February 20, 2002

The advent of the present year brought along with it one heartening bit of news. After a long gap of five years, the reconstituted Indian Board for Wildlife (IBWL), the highest body in the country established for laying down policy and issuing directives for proper management of Protected Areas, finally held its 21st meeting in January.

To say the least, it was indeed ironic that during these past five years, while wildlife and forests located across the entire country were being subjected to innumerable threats ranging from the small-time poacher to globally funded development projects, the people who really matter for the good of wildlife, were unable to put their heads together under this august forum.

But, without going into the reasons that were responsible for this long gap, it should now be optimistically hoped that the IBWL has delved deeply into the issues that it was faced with, and will would now further ensure that each priority area that it identified in the resolutions it passed, gets a balanced priority, without one impinging upon another. This attains great importance when the process of actual implementation of a number of policy decisions, tends to come up against some inherent contradictions.

The 18 resolutions passed at the IBWL meeting encompass the entire range of issues facing wildlife in the country. These include the important decision that wildlife and forests shall be declared a priority sector at the national level, for which adequate funds should be earmarked. It has also been resolved that law enforcement agencies must ensure that poachers and traders in illicit wildlife products are given quick and deterrent punishment.

The revenue earning potential of wildlife tourism has been acknowledged, but its development should be done in a way that does not have adverse impact on wildlife or protected areas. This revenue component should be used entirely to augment available resources for conservation.

Since there is an inbuilt contradiction in managing PA's, while at the same time protecting the interests of the villagers and tribals living around these areas, the IBWL resolution has urged that this issue be handled with sensitivity and with maximum possible participation of the affected people. It has been suggested that they should have access to the minor forest produce from forests outside of national parks and sanctuaries, and also be provided with opportunities that help them maintain a symbiotic relationship with the forests and wildlife.

The positive role of NGO's involved in conservation has been stressed upon and it has been resolved that these be given greater governmental as well as societal recognition and support, while mainstream media has been asked to highlight both the activities of the NGOs, as well as the successes of governmental initiatives that have worked.

A resolution that may have far-reaching benefits is the one which outlines that there would be no diversion of forest land for non-forest purposes, from critical and ecologically fragile wildlife habitats. This is aimed at countering the increasing threats wild habitats face from mega projects in the power or irrigation sectors. As a corollary it has also been resolved that land falling within 10 km of the boundaries of national parks and sanctuaries should be notified as eco-fragile zones under provisions contained in the Environment (Protection) Act and Rules.

Other resolutions cover such important administrative issues as removal of encroachments and illegal activities from within forest lands and PA's, a ban on plantations of commercial mono-culture to replace natural forests, and ensuring that the settlement of rights in national parks and sanctuaries should not be used to exclude or reduce the areas that are crucial to, and an integral part of the wildlife habitat.

Perhaps the most important indicator for the need for the IBWL to pull up its socks came when its Chairman, the Prime Minister summed up his address with, "Lastly, I would like all of us to resolve that we shall end the relative neglect of wildlife conservation in recent years. To begin with, this Board should meet more often. All of us have many other tasks and concerns to attend to. And they too are important. However, wildlife conservation is too important a task to be treated lightly or ritualistically".

One hopes that his message is loud and clear.

WILDLIFE MANAGEMENT NEEDS RAPID RESPONSE UNITS

February 6, 2002

One of the primary prerequisites of good wildlife management is the deployment of rapid response units at key points, which should be geared to tackle sudden emergencies that may crop up at any time in our national parks or wildlife sanctuaries. Most of these emergencies have their genesis in cases arising out of man-animal conflicts, which have tended to increase with shrinking wild habitats, and encroachments into forests by the burgeoning human population living on peripheral areas.

Unfortunately, our wildlife management agencies were recently found wanting in two recent incidents which occurred almost simultaneously – one in Bijnor forest division of Uttar Pradesh and the second in the Rajaji national park in Uttaranchal.

In the first case, a young leopard was found trapped in a wire noose set up by a poacher in the forests of Bijnor district. Considering that the leopard was alive when discovered, it is obvious that the noose was not fatal, and all that was immediately required was to immobilise him with a dart, and set him loose. But darting needs a tranquilizer gun, which was not available with the department at that time. By the time it was procured, sufficient time had elapsed for the leopard to injure himself in his struggle to get free, and that necessitated him to be transported to Lucknow for veterinary attention. Coupled with the injuries that he sustained in the trap, the trauma of transportation from Bijnore to Lucknow in a truck was enough to kill him by the time he arrived.

In the second incident that occurred on the night of 24-25 January, a train hit an elephant calf on the railway line between Haridwar and Motichur railway stations in Kharkhari beat of Rajaji national park. The impact of the accident did not kill the calf immediately, but tossed him next to the railway line, injured and immobilised. The distraught mother elephant refused to budge from his side, and all efforts to distract her by noise or a water cannon remained futile.

Again, what was needed here was to tranquillize her, so that a vet could approach the calf, and attend to his injuries. However, in this case too, the tranquilizer gun was unavailable since the Wildlife Institute of India vet – the only person who could have been called on to dart the elephant, was out of town with the gun, to perform duty at the Republic Day parade in Delhi in which elephants and other animals were participating. In the absence of any other wildlife trained vet in the Rajaji national park, vital time was lost and the calf succumbed to his injuries.

Both these incidents are indicative of the urgent need for the forest departments of both states to review the response time that they take to handle wildlife crises that arise in their respective spheres of control.

The state of Uttaranchal, with its valued possession of huge forest tracts, more than 100 tigers, several hundred leopards and elephants, should not dither in procuring trained wildlife vets and an adequate number of tranquilizer guns to meet such eventualities in the future.

Closer home, the events leading to the death of that leopard trapped in Bijnor, and more recently the death of the chimpanzee in the Lucknow Zoo, are stark reminders that we still have a very long way to go

A TRIBUTE TO RAMBHA - THE ELEPHANT

January 16 & 30, 2001

*When I mentioned two famous tigers of Corbett national park earlier in these columns, I was pleasantly surprised by some very evocative responses from readers who recalled the good old days when these tigers were the pride of Corbett. Heartened by these responses, I am moved to recount the story of the famous Corbett elephant **Rambha** and her mahout **Ishtiaq**, which was published soon after she died.....*

The tiger had moved deep into the elephant grass, and it now seemed difficult to dislodge him from there. Although we could still see him indistinctly, a deep nullah prevented us from going any nearer for that vital photograph that I still hadn't been able to get. It was here that the intricate combination of mahout and elephant revealed itself. Ishtiaq, the mahout, motioned to me to stay ready with my camera, while his toes sent silent directives to Rambha, the elephant.

In response, the snaking trunk lifted a huge clod of wet mud and sent it flying across the dividing nullah, landing in a spray on the recalcitrant tiger. Alarmed, or probably angry at this ignominy, out he came roaring in a mock charge, canines fully bared. For those few moments the humans clearly perceived the terror that strikes a tiger's prey. It may have lasted seconds, but was enough to freeze our blood. Thankfully, the fingers worked away in reflex to give our cameras the everlasting impressions of a charging tiger. "**Wah wah Ishtiaq, wah Rambha wah, shabaash!**" went the rounds of congratulations and thanksgiving, showered excitedly on the mahout and his charge, following this magnificent sighting of the elusive tiger.

Ishtiaq and Rambha, Rambha and Ishtiaq. A combination in which there were no peers. For all serious visitors to the famous Corbett National Park, a ride into the forests with Ishtiaq is a unique experience. An excellent tracker, he deftly reads the signs left by the denizens of the forest from atop his lofty perch on Rambha's neck. And if during the ride, the situation does not warrant absolute silence, in his own inimitable style and dialect, he will give you a lesson or two in jungle lore that you are not likely to find in any book. Being the most sought-after pair in Corbett, he and his elephant have perforce taken many a pompous VIP into the forest, but for the average wildlife enthusiast, Ishtiaq is the VIP, easily striking a balance of camaraderie and strictness with the tourists while out on his two excursions each day.

I have had the privilege of being a close friend of Ishtiaq ever since my visits to Corbett started in 1985. Initially going out with any mahout that happened to be allotted to me, I gradually learnt to distinguish between the good ones and the average. This process of elimination finally resulted in short-listing a couple of mahouts like Nazir and Nawab. And of course, Ishtiaq. The top slot, however, went easily to Ishtiaq because of his elephant, Rambha. She was sure-footed and steady on all kinds of terrain. Right from the time one started off from camp astride her, one felt brave and confident of facing the tiger on its own ground. Never known to have backed off or panicked, she easily conveyed her confidence to the riders through her studied nonchalance during tiger sightings. Even if there were no sightings of the big cat, the ride itself was always eventful. And so, year after year I returned to Corbett for the inevitable rendezvous with my human and pachyderm friend.

Recently preoccupied by frequent visits to Bandhavgarh and Kanha national parks, I had been unable to find time to go to Corbett for almost two years. Blaming myself for this lapse in loyalty for my most favourite forest, I finally squeezed in a trip to Corbett during end-January. The thrill of reaching Dhikala camp was as exhilarating as ever. The welcoming hugs from the modest staff members were so warm that they dispelled the biting cold of the season. But tragic news was at hand. "Rambha is dying," they told me. It was shocking and unbelievable. Elephants have long lives, we've been told. How could she die, she was only seventy?

We made a beeline for the place where Rambha was lying sick and helpless. The very first sight of the fallen giant made me falter. She was lying on her left side. The ground where she lay had been scraped and muddied by her vain efforts to stand upright. A bonfire was burning nearby to ward off the cold from her, as well as the humans attending on her. There was Ishtiaq, his wife and children, the Range Officer, and a motley group of other mahouts and characuts. All had genuine concern on their faces. An elephant for a mahout is not an animal but a family member. And here, a family member was dying.

Ishtiaq and I met each other without speaking. The signs were all too evident to warrant speech. We walked up to where her head lay, and sat down close to her. The only eye visible on that gaunt face followed us. While I stroked her feeble trunk, Ishtiaq reached out and wiped the trickling discharge from under her eye. " *Na beta, mat ro. Bahut dard ho raha hai?*" he asked. I also felt the start of a trickle on my face that needed wiping, and I did that furtively.

Later, sitting on a charpoy near the blazing fire where Rambha lay, I finally managed to piece together the events that were about to deprive Corbett National Park of one of its most well-known treasures.

Soon after Corbett Park closed for the monsoons last year, a wild tusker started making frequent forays into the Dhikala encampment. Probably emboldened by the lack of tourist activity, or maybe spurred on by the enticing smell of the female riding elephants in the camp, he repeatedly targeted the *filkhana* or stables where the elephants were quartered. More often than not, he was driven off before he could actually enter, but on 16th July, he managed to sneak in, and in the ensuing melee, drove a tusk into Rambha's right ear. The wound was not severe, but took time to heal. During treatment, she was quartered at Ramnagar from where she returned to Dhikala in November, in time for the start of another busy tourist season. But not being certified fully fit by the vet, she remained off duty.

It was on the fateful night of 24th November that the wild tusker raided the *filkhana* again. Probably out of panic because of her last encounter with him, she jerked frantically at the hobble-chain restraining her hind leg, breaking it with sheer effort. The commotion culminated with the Range Officer firing in the air and scaring off the tusker. But in the effort of breaking the chain, something in Rambha's leg snapped too. According to Ishtiaq, it was not a broken bone, nor even a dislocation. It was some vital nerve that suffered a traumatic injury, resulting in the leg getting inflamed and bloated out of all proportion.

Getting to work with his indigenous and native remedies, Ishtiaq treated and nursed her leg for almost one month. Rambha showed signs of recovery, the inflammation on her leg subsided, but she didn't attain full fitness. She was checked up on 21st January by doctors from Pantnagar, who prescribed tonics and calcium tablets to speed up her recovery. But that probably was not ordained. She stopped eating her rations from the next day, despite all efforts from her human friends to coerce or force-feed her.

Six days of starvation for an ailing elephant took their toll, and on 27th morning, she fell down heavily on her face. That, according to Ishtiaq, was an ominous sign. All her desperate efforts to get up, even with the support of the puny human hands, sapped whatever little energy that may have been left in her emaciated frame. Nayyar, a forest department staffer, gave her two bottles of intravenous glucose, but it was already too late. By the time I arrived at Dhikala at noon, all hopes had been lost, and when I sat down near her with Ishtiaq, we were just two of a group of helpless onlookers, desolately awaiting the passing of a forest giant.

While we sat near her late into the night, Rambha's death throes continued. She kept writhing and stretching her legs again and again. Each movement resulted in a discharge of urine, indicating that her sphincter muscles had succumbed to the weakness. But not once did she utter a sound. When Irfan, her characut pushed in a lump of gur into her mouth, she weakly but firmly twirled her trunk around his arm and clearly told him not to do that. And so, all that her human retinue could do was to stoke the fire to keep it burning warmly, and to keep adjusting the huge cotton gadda that was her protection from the night dew, and which repeatedly kept falling off her jerky, twitching body.

Before retiring for the night, I stroked her gently for the last time, and promised myself that I would not come near her again, and thus avoid seeing her in mortal agony. The thrill of coming to Corbett had transformed into sadness, and even the sighting of a magnificent male tiger that crossed from under the Dhikala machan, had failed to dissipate the gloom. Next morning, I was told that she spent the night in great discomfort, and that the road gang labourers had now been requisitioned to start digging the pit that would be her grave. Not feeling brave enough to face the end, I came away from Dhikala, foolishly confident that I had left her alive, and hoping that she just might survive after all.

Since then, I have had one thing uppermost on my mind. I wanted everyone who knew and loved Rambha to know about her passing, but the hope for the miracle to happen kept alive. The dreaded news however arrived on 4th February when Suresh Pant, a Dhikala staff member, came to visit me.

Rambha died at 8.45 PM on 28th of January 1998. Her gaunt body now rests within the Dhikala camp, at the very spot where she had fallen down to breathe her last.

Ishtiaq's companion of fourteen years, and the favourite of countless Indian and foreign wildlife enthusiasts, has finally passed on to the Happy Hunting Grounds.

*P.S. Subsequently, this article was included in my book **'Ankush Days – the story of Ishtiaq mahout of Corbett Tiger Reserve'***

It is available at www.amazon.in/dp/8194798035